Parents:
What are they good for?

Benjamin DeCasseres

STAND ALONE
SA1252

Parents: What Are They Good For?
By Benjamin DeCasseres, 1916

PUBLIC DOMAIN

Originally published in:

Revolt Vol. I No.1
(January 1, 1916)
New York, NY

This edition ©2023 Nine-Banded Books

Nine-Banded Books
Post Office Box 1862
Charleston, WV 25327
U.S.A.

NineBandedBooks.com

ISBN: 978-1-7356438-6-1

Frontispiece: George Grosz, *Family (Familie)*
from the illustrated book *Ecce Homo*, 1916,
published 1922–23

"Bookend" illustrations expropriated from
Gelet Burgess's *Goops and How to Be Them*,
published 1900

Published in association with Union of Egoists

STAND ALONE SA1252

CONTENTS

Parents: What Are They Good for?
~9~

Revolt Volume I, Number 1
(facsimile)
~94~

Publisher's Postscript
~105~

Author Profile
~117~

Parents: What Are They Good For?

Parents: What Are They Good For?
(1916)

WE are in the midst of a revolution of women. It is almost an accomplished fact. But in the great movements, economic and sexual, which are going on all over the world, there is on more revolution to be accomplished.

We are in the midst of a revolution of women. It is almost an accomplished fact. But in the great movements, economic and sexual, which are going on all over the world, there is one more revolution to be accomplished.

It is the revolt of the children against their parents. And that will be the most tremendous, the sublimest revolution of all.

It is the revolt of the children against their parents. And that will be the most tremendous, the sublimest revolution of all.

It is time the truth was uttered about parents and their attitude toward those they bring into the world by an act of passion. It is time the mask of sentimental lies surrounding the sacredness of parents was slit into a thousand pieces and tossed back into the wardrobe-room of race-fakes.

It is time the truth was uttered about parents and their attitude toward those they bring into the world by an act of passion. It is time the mask of sentimental lies surrounding the sacredness of parents was slit into a thousand pieces and tossed back into the wardrobe-room of race-fakes.

Parents: What are they good for?

Parents: What are they good for?

Let every man and woman look into the last recesses of his heart and answer that question fully.

Let every man and woman look into the last recesses of his heart and answer that question fully.

Parents: What are they good for?

Parents: What are they good for?

Let the squeezed, mutilated, shabby, humdrum, aching days of millions of youths and girls stand up and answer unashamedly.

Let the squeezed, mutilated, shabby, humdrum, aching days of millions of youths and girls stand up and answer unashamedly.

Parents: Waht are they good for?

Parents: What are they good for?

And billions of strangled, mutilated Minds and Passions and millions of shabby Days rise out of their tombs and answer: They should have been hanged before we grew into our sixth year.

And billions of strangled, mutilated Minds and Passions and millions of shabby Days rise out of their tombs and answer: They should have been hanged before we grew into our sixth year.

Parents: Or the Mania for Mutilation. Millions of human beings might write a thesis with that for a title—a thesis that would make the horrors of a Dostoievsky seem merely a charivari.

Parents: Or the Mania for Mutilation. Millions of human beings might write a thesis with that for a title—a thesis that would make the horrors of a Dostoievsky seem merely a charivari.

Veiled beneath that vaunted sacred love of father and mother there lies a mania for mutilation which for pure diabolism is nowhere matched in nature.

Veiled beneath that vaunted sacred love of father and mother there lies a mania for mutilation which for pure diabolism is nowhere matched in nature.

Under the guise of a perpetual act of self-sacrifice the mother becomes the most incurably selfish being that nature has yet created. Motherhood is nature's supreme diabolistic paradox.

Under the guise of a perpetual act of self-sacrifice the mother becomes the most incurably selfish being that nature has yet created. Motherhood is nature's supreme diabolistic paradox.

It is always herself she fights for, and never for the child. It is always herself she dies for, and never for the sake of the child. Her love is the very frenzy and insanity of possession.

It is always herself she fights for, and never for that child. It is always herself she dies for, and never for the sake of the child. Her love is the very frenzy and insanity of possession.

The father is greater than the mother, because his love-greed in regard to the offspring is not so cruel. Some father will even concede the right of a child to have opinions, ideas and sensations of its own. Motherhood can never ascend to that. It remains forever in the sties of self-worship.

The father is greater than the mother, because his love-greed in regard to the offspring is not so cruel. Some father will even concede the right of a child to have opinions, ideas and sensations of its own. Motherhood can never ascend to that. It remains forever in the sties of self-worship.

Most children are born into a home. And by home I mean a death-cell. At the moment of birth the murderous machinations of the parents begin. Variation from the parent-type is the one thing to be feared. Hence the home. Hence the squirt-guns of stability, feigned godliness and prudery which begin their work on the senses and brain of the child just born. And when he first begins to smell it is the rotten stench of sanctity that greets his nostrils.

Most children are born into a home. And by home I mean a death-cell. At the moment of birth the murderous machinations of the parents begin. Variation from the parent-type is the one thing to be feared. Hence the home. Hence the squirt-guns of respectability, feigned godliness and prudery which begin their work on the sense and brain of the child just born. And when he first begins to smell it is the rotten stench of sanctity that greets his nostrils.

I accuse all parents of being liars every second in every hour in every day of their lives in the presence of their children.

I accuse all parents of being liars every second in every hour in every day of their lives in the presence of their children.

I accuse every parent of a pantomime of hypocritical mummery from the day a child is born unto them.

I accuse every parent of a pantomime of hypocritical mummery from the day a child is born unto them.

I accuse every parent of conspiring against the unique vision and temperament that is born unto them.

I accuse every parent of conspiring against the unique vision and temperament that is born unto them.

I accuse every parent of spiritual mental, physical murder in seeking to gag the soul of the new-born and to mould it in the image of one or both of them.

I accuse every parent of spiritual, mental, physical murder in seeking to gag the soul of the newborn and to mould it in the image of one or both of them.

I accuse every parent of cowardice before the wide-open look of the child. They fake their personality from the very moment the child looks at them.

I accuse every parent of spiritual, mental, physical murder in seeking to gag the soul of the newborn and to mould it in the image of one or both of them.

I accuse every parent of cowardice before the wide-open look of the child. They fake their personality from the very moment the child looks at them.

I accuse every parent of cowardice before the wide-open look of the child. They fake their personality from the very moment the child looks at them.

(No child ever knew its parents. No parent ever knew his or her child.)

(No child ever knew its parents. No parent ever knew his or her child.)

I accuse parents of every physical and mental anguish that boys and girls suffer between the ages of thirteen and twenty.

I accuse parents of every physical and mental anguish that boys and girls suffer between the ages of thirteen and twenty.

(If parents only knew of the hate that enforced virgins feel for their parents, whose licentious and unrestrained practices in the marriage bond have obliterated their own early hatreds for their own parents.)

(If parents only knew of the hate that enforced virgins feel for their parents, whose licentious and unrestrained practices in the marriage bond have obliterated their own early hatreds for their own parents.)

The home, the parent, must be protected at all costs!

The home, the parent, must be protected at all costs!

Does a "girl "go wrong" (that is, does she dare assert the rights of her womanhood and seek sanity away from the insane asylum for perverts called the respectable home?) The first thought in the minds of father and mother is the disgrace that will fall on THEM. A girl—a thing of flesh and blood—is being sacrificed to the Moloch of Respectability for the sake of the parents, those unrestrained and licentious parents, safe in the bosom of the marriage license!

Does a girl "go wrong" (that is, does she dare assert the rights of her womanhood and seek sanity away from the insane asylum for perverts called the respectable home?) The first thought in the minds of father and mother is the disgrace that will fall on THEM. A girl—a thing of flesh and blood—is being sacrificed to the Moloch of Respectability for the sake of the parents, those unrestrained and licentious parents, safe in the bosom of the marriage license!

The girl "went wrong"? No. The girl went right. Better one year of full surrender to love and passion and then death in the river than a life of respectable virginity and its inferno of agonies.

The girl "went wrong"? No. The girl went right. Better one year of full surrender to love and passion and then death in the river than a life of respectable virginity and its inferno of agonies.

Does a boy "go wrong"? He gambles, he drinks, he seduces, he steals. Again the shriek through the cracking walls and falling roof of the House of Dies. "Our reputation! Our reputation! My God! Our reputation!"—that is the cry that mounts to the ironic tomcat squat on the tottering chimney.

Does a boy "go wrong"? He gambles, he drinks, he seduces, he steals. Again the shriek through the cracking walls and falling roof of the House of Lies. "Our reputation! Our reputation! My God! Our reputation!"—that is the cry that mounts to the ironic tomcat squat on the tottering chimney.

No parent ever showed sufficient respect for the child. Love—yes. Respect—never. That is because the love of the parent is the veil of selfishness and egotism, and respect involves self-sacrifice, an abasement in their own eyes of their supreme importance, a division of power.

No parent ever showed sufficient respect for the child. Love—yes. Respect—never. That is because the love of the parent is the veil of selfishness and egotism, and respect involves self-sacrifice, an abasement in their own eyes of their supreme importance, a division of power.

Love is easier than respect and reaps a richer harvest of lies. To love a child involves no effort. To respect a child one must have ascended high in the scale of emotional and intellectual development.

Love is easier than respect and reaps a richer harvest of lies. To love a child involves no effort. To respect a child one must have ascended high in the scale of emotional and intellectual development.

The parent has no rights which the child is bound to respect. It is in the world without its own consent, bringing with it all the ills that flesh and mind are heir to.

The parent has no rights which the child is bound to respect. It is in the world without its own consent, bringing with it all the ills that flesh and mind are heir to.

Ancestors, environment, parents stand at the cradle like a menace of death. The social and economic systems under which a child is born have no rights which the child is bound to respect.

Ancestors, environment, parents stand at the cradle like a menace of death. The social and economic systems under which a child is born have no rights which the child is bound to respect.

A mere flesh and blood asset of the parent and the blood sucking social and religious⸻ts, which the child is shot—what should the spect?

A mere flesh and blood asset of the parent and the blood sucking social and religious system for which the child is shot—what should the child respect?

ITS OWN SOUL ONLY!

ITS OWN SOUL ONLY!

The revolution of the child! The new Children's Crusade! This time they will march to rescue their own souls from the Unholy Sepulchre of their infidel parents.

The revolution of the child! The new Children's Crusade! This time they will march to rescue their own souls from the Unholy Sepulchre of their infidel parents.

Youths and maidens and children, you must soon write your Marseillaise. Stifled ones, strangled ones, mutilated ones, dutiful ones, suckled in the House of Fear and raised in the House of Craven Respectability or Leprous Poverty, the time approaches when each and every one must ask the heart:

Youths and maidens and children, you must soon write your Marseillaise. Stifled ones, strangled ones, mutilated ones, dutiful ones, suckled in the House of Fear and raised in the House of Craven Respectability or Leprous Poverty, the time approaches when each and every one must ask the heart:

My parents: What are they good for?

My parents: What are they good for?

And your hearts will answer: Good for nothing until they are taught to respect, honor and obey us!

And your hearts will answer: Good for nothing until they are taught to respect, honor and obey us!

BENJAMIN DE CASSERES.

Benjamin DeCasseres

"What Are You

Going to Do?"

REVOLT
Volume I, Number 1
(January 1, 1916)

~FACSIMILE~

To the Militants in the Labor Movement

¶ The REVOLT will receive gladly and will print free of charge reports on strikes, on demonstrations or any activity among the workers.

¶ Meetings and demonstrations will be announced free in the columns of the REVOLT.

EVOË

BE greeted, carrier of glad tidings, fulfiller of our hopes: Glory be to Thee—New Year. Born amidst destruction, destiny chose Thee to crown the work of demolition. Thou art the herald of a greater cataclysm, the stormy petrel of the approaching Social Revolution.

With pleasure we part from Thine illustrious father. In his reign the cancer of smoot opportunism burst open, revealing the pitiful sight of decaying impotent ideas. Gladly we follow to the burial ground Messrs. Compromise and Common Sense.

At last we can breathe again. Caught in the maelstrom of greed and envy, Madame Evolution disappears, leaving the battle-field to the children of Revolt.

Ye rebels do not whine over the downfall of capitalistic culture and civilization. A new world is being born before your very eyes. A cataclysm has cleared the air and freshness is filling our lungs.

Discredited are the corrupters of revolutionary ideas. Disrobed they stand before us. Their masks torn down, they show their face in all hideousness and shamelessness. The International is not dead. Humanity is not dead—dead are only the false prophets. Like rats they are hurrying from the sinking vessel carrying their torn mantles on lame shoulders.

O yes, they had arranged everything nicely. Step by step they entered the morgue of capitalism. Accepting the bread crumbs from the table of the exploiters and rulers they grew into the system and became partners of the masters. How practical they imagined to be! How they smiled at the utopian dreamers, those who couldn't sell their vision, their heart, their soul to the highest bidder. They knew better. Participating in the capitalistic corruption, selling their brain, becoming prostitutes, these means they intended to establish Free

roud they were when they succeeded in selling their first offspring to a bourgeois publication. They didn't want to sell their soul, oh, no! What they wanted was to reach a larger public.

Lo, behold the result! The poisoned fruit of popularity took hold of their brain. They started as popularizers and ended as vulgarizers of ideas. Fortunately, the minotaurus caught them ere they had chance to pollute the child of the future. *Requiescat in pâce.*

Ye militant rebels, you who are disgusted with the pettiness of dull-headed leaders, political climbers and criers on public marts, THE REVOLT greets you.

Ye workers—submerged in the daily task of economic slavery, embittered by the everlasting struggle for daily bread, THE REVOLT greets you.

Ye down trodden and disheartened, ye outcasts, wherever you may hide yourself, THE REVOLT greets you.

Ye coiners of new shapes, strugglers for new impressions, THE REVOLT greets you.

Ye impractical dreamers scattered all over the continent, THE REVOLT greets you.

Ye lonesome souls crying in the wilderness of our barbaric civilization for friendship and sympathy, THE REVOLT greets you.

Ye searchers for truth and light, living in blessed obscurity, THE REVOLT greets you.

Ye All, workers in clay, in colors, in words, workers on the sea and workers in the bosom of our mother Earth, ye who contemplate and ye who produce, THE REVOLT greets you.

Neither intellectual snobs nor horny-hand philophers you will find in our ranks: rebels against exploitation of men by men, rebels against domination from whatever direction they may come, rebels against the State of Capitalism, rebels in art, science and literature, ry Revolters in Revolt we are.

Have you a message? You are welcome

... we repeat, the
friends of the Social War
a tremendous sexual transit...   need a
publication which states in   ....
and fearless manner.

To succeed in our mission, we .... sitate be
proclaim our enmity to all the w ......names, and
hypocrisies in contemporary life. THE REVOLT will
be the voice of the conscious rebels and it will not
shrink from the duty of exposing all compromises
and underhand dealings which disgrace the labor
movement of this country.

THE REVOLT will have no sympathy with ex-revolutionists, ex-idealists, common-sense-men, sneaks, cowards, and business men, gents who use the "horny hand" for the purpose of climbing to a higher position in the capitalist society; those who are revolutionists in theory and reactionists in practice. The conscious workingman is tired of wise, practical, matter-of-fact climbers.

THE REVOLT will not be tolerant. Our whole social, political, and artistic life is corrupted by the philosophy of tolerance—the philosophy of the mollusc. THE REVOLT will not walk hand-in-hand with the dear, good, sympathizers, the mock golden-rule people, who say neither yea nor nay, men who preach harmony between capital and labor, those who never want to hurt the enemy.

THE REVOLT will have little sympathy with the man of common sense. Common sense is a good quality for a horse dealer or a bond broker, but out of place in the revolutionary movement. It will not pave the way for the social upheaval.

And first, last, and all the time, THE REVOLT will have nothing but a good dose of contempt for those sweet æsthetes who "see beauty everywhere."

The days of charlatans and political upstarts are numbered. The American workingman begins to realize the truth of the slogan: The emancipation of the working class must be accomplished by the workers themselves. "Scientific" socialism, political inanity, and pure-and-simple unionism have not been able to paralyze the whole energy of Labor. All the labor revolts seen in the last few years have proved the value of direct action and prepared the way for the final goal: The overthrow of the exploiting system through the Social General Strike.

THE REVOLT will not compromise with Utopians, those who believe that in order to be able to revolutionize economic conditions, the proletariat must first win political power, those who transplant the center of rebellion from the factory to the Congress, from the street to the broker's office; those who have transformed economic revolutionary socialism into a political reform movement. In their Utopian attempt to smuggle in the Social Revolution under the cover of reform, they have succeeded only in transforming themselves into pure and simple politicians. Their position depends on voters and not on revolutionary .... ation in the politics .... ce be ... of Utopianism.

We are on the threshold of an upheaval of greater dimensions than any former uprising, a dead awakening between the oppressed and the oppressor, a struggle that will truly justify the statement remark of Carlyle, "the account day of a thousand years."

THE REVOLT is the clarion of a rebellious army, the harbinger of future victory. Do not let us hesitate to be true to ourselves. Let us walk the straight road and state our ideas boldly and fearlessly. The judgment and opinion of political upstarts, harlots, and philistines cannot teach us. The man of common sense, the golden-rule simpleton, and the philistine will continue in their denunciation of the Extremist. Let them!

CHOP!

FROM eighteen years to fifty the Intellectual Proletarian ate bread and water and slept in the garret which was his laboratory.

From eighteen to fifty the Intellectual Proletarian wore rags and shivered in winters.

From eighteen to fifty the Intellectual Proletarian deprived himself of all that lightens life in order to bend the longer over his test tubes.

At fifty the process was completed—a wonderful process of inestimable value to the world.

Thereupon a Capitalist, after a languid ten minutes meditation, took the process and turned it into millions. And having stored his millions he kindly remembered the Intellectual Proletarian with the shreds of his nightingale tongue pie and meltings of his most delicate ices.

And the Intellectual Proletarian as he sat in his place (which was only a little below that of the favored lackeys) devoured the scraps and swelled with gratitude.

And he chanted gratefully:

"Oh, beneficent capitalist!
Oh, generous and far-seeing Capitalist!
Oh, wisest and best of all human kind!
Till the day of my death let me celebrate your kindness and wisdom!
Let me megaphone your praises to the farth constellation!"

CONCLUSION.

Boy, get me a guillotine and a half-do... Intellectual Proletarians.

HORA*

The greatest disadvantage of the much glorified, lies in the expenditure civilization. It is mainly ... are sacrificed, those who promote posterity. —NIETZSCHE.

REV... ...LISHING ASSOCIA...ON
...East 107th Street   New York, N. Y.

Hippolyte Havel, Editor
Jack Isaacson, Secretary   Gussie Miller, Treasurer

Subscription:
Yearly . . . . One Dollar
Six months . . . . 50 cents
Three months . . . . . . 25 cents

Application for entry as second class mater at the post office at New York pending.

Observations

Our Friends on Trial

CAPLAN and Schmidt are fighting for their lives. A ferocious enemy with a big capital behind him is making the most strenuous effort to garotte two militant members of the working class. Comrades, do not let us use big words but let us save our friends. Our protest must be heard all over the country. Caplan and Schmidt are energetic, conscious rebels, blood of our blood, flesh of our flesh. No mistaken zeal for the welfare of crafty labor leaders on the part of a Clarence Darrow or a Lincoln Steffens will be able to break the defence of Schmidt or Caplan. If we do not succeed in destroying the conspiracy of the Manufacturers Association other men in the militant labor movement will be selected as victims.

Balzac on Joe Hill

THERE are many doubting Thomases in the movement; ever ready to approve of and to believe in any gossip or slander about comrades who happen to have a prominent position in public life on account of their ability, these doubting chechakoes are ever sceptical when the time arrives to defend these very same men and women. Their mental horizon is obscured by porkchop philosophy.

To-day they doubt the defence of Joe Hill. They ...ot grasp such a situation. A social rebel sacri... his life for a mere woman! Thus they prove ...ation of their vision.

...ntains more romance than any romantic ...eproduce. Friends, spare a few moments ...ous time for the reading of Honore de ...try Doctor." Here you have the case ...inatory predicted by the greatest ...Nineteenth Century. Instead of ...enton, the Dark Lady of Shake... Harris and G. Bernard Shaw ... the case of the mysterious

in A..ica, neither ha.. .. nor have the hypocritical ..at Indian Revolution; they ... And now we are to believe ..ica and Asia are solely due to ...at naive idiocy!

So far the ... ..a exploiters and robbers succeeded in suppressing all uprising among the "lower races." But since they have started a big massacre among themselves at home the natives have a chance to rise en masse. Those European benefactors and their mercenaries, whether they be Germans, English, Dutch or Italians, will now reap a rich harvest in empty pockets and broken skulls.

Let us express our wish: Filipinos, join the Asiatic and African Befreiungskrieg and drive the Yankees from your hearth and home!

A Bloody Traitor

WHAT every observer of Chinese Affairs knew long ago became visible to the average citizen to-day: Yuan Shi Kai, the Bastard-Manchu-Bannerman, succeeded in his nefarious plan to strangle the Chinese Republic. Under his tutelage it was only a Shadow Republic, now even the Shadow disappeared. Traitor to the old Dynasty, traitor to his benefactress, the old sly Empress Dowager, traitor to the Revolution, the crafty Taleyrand of our day tore at last down his mask of neutral benevolence. But will he succeed in escaping his fate? His days are counted.

In Memoriam

WE all knew that he was doomed. With heart-rending anxiety we watched the progress of the fatal disease. No whe is gone. The I. W. W. lost one of their staunchest friends and defenders.

Joseph O'Brien was hardly known to the rank and file outside of New York City. But the boys in New York will mourn deeply the loss of "Joe."

For O'Brien was not a mere sympathizer. He was with his whole heart and soul in the labor movement. By active participation in the strikes in Lawrence and Paterson, and especially during the memorable agitation of the unemployed the past winter, O'Brien proved his intense sincerity with the social rebellion. Day or night, at any hour, Joe was always willing and ready to assist the boys who happened to fall in the clutches of the guardians of inequality. To the last days of his earthly journey he kept his interest in the agitation. When I saw him last in the hospital he expressed his wish to see Elzabeth Gurly Flynn and Carl Tresca.

His hospitality was unbounded. Many happy hours we used to spend in Joe's cherful surroundings, discussing, fighting over theories, and I fear, sometimes making Mary's life miserable. It must

a rather diff... d for h... ...o
...vel in the upper rooms while a
went on down below.

Joseph O'Brien was a native son of Virginia and he possessed the charming manners of a truly cultured man, not the traditional politeness of the sword-buckling southern gentleman but the inborn, inherent politeness of a noble soul. So little are we used to natural chivalry that I remember vividly how embarrassed I felt when I met "Joe" for the first time.

A splendid career on the capitalistic press was open for him. He could have had a prominent position in the journalistic world. He was one of the strongest men in Hearst's newspaper syndicate. The organization of the Boston *Journal* was his work. But unlike many of his confreres he soon found out the corruption of the press. The spirit of revolt took hold of his soul. He left the unholy temple of public prostitution. He gave up everything and became a bold free-lance.

The social rebels lost a good comrade.

Another Fighter Gone

ED LEWIS died in the accursed city of Los Angeles. Ed was a remarkable personality. His position in the labor movement in this country was unique. Kicked out from the ranks of the F. of L., kicked out from S. P., kicked out from the I. W. W., bitterly attacked by Anarchists, he kept up an agitation on his own hook. In the middle age he surely would have held the position of a *condottieri* or a landsknecht in one of the numerous armies of freebooters.

THE REVOLT does not swear to the old adage: *de mortuis nil nisi bonum*. Yet we can not help to give a devil his due. Ed Lewis had many sincere, ay, fanatical friends and admirers, friends who stuck to him no matter what escapades he may have committed. Such a man must possess a strong individuality.

Ed was a forceful stump speaker. Very few men in the revolutionary ranks can hold an open air audience so spell bound as Lewis did. Those of us who had the opportunity to meet him in private appreciated certain qualities in him which remained hidden to the rank and file at large.

Anarchist Forum
For Current Topics

Meets every Sunday at 8 p. m., at the Ferrer Center, 63 East 107th Street, New York.

Discussions will be opened:

JANUARY	-	Harry Kelly
FEBRUARY	-	Leonard D. Abbott
MARCH	-	Hippolyte Havel
APRIL	-	Gussie Miller

The Outcast

I am cast out,
I feel it—
In bitterness I wander
I am cast out
And from the world I cannot hide.
Though cast out
To the whole world I belong.
When I have least
They have me most.
Those who most give
The least receive.
I am in anger,
I hate—
A wandering outcast I am.
I sorrow,
I wander,
My heart with silence is locked,
And without tears I weep.

* * *

They know me not,
But some there are
Whose tears like mine inwardly fall
And I feel them
If I see them not,
I am full of speech,
And dumb I must be.
Most are they who laughter hear
And we love,
And their sight is with darkness veiled.
I am cast out,
Though I wander to lose myself,
All eyes upon me I feel.
I wander,
But sorrow grips me,
And anger wakes me.

* * *

The burden hours ring away,
Morning goes to night.
Between I wander,
And I cannot lose my own self.
I am outcast—
My silence speaks,
And there are who hear when they feel.
I am cast out,
I wander,
Midst six millions I wander,
And more lonely than on the prairie I feel.
The people heedless move,
And how still they stand.
So ring the hours away,
So go the days by,
On the time I wander,
I am outcast.

MAX WEBER.

The Office of the Revolt Raided by the Police

ALTHOUGH great believers in amorphism we have no intention to remove the office of THE REVOLT each month to a different locality. In truth, our great desire was to locate the office in the center of the town. Alas, we did not take into consideration the benevolent and protecting attitude of the police towards the revolutionary movement in general and towards the group Revolt in particular. Ere the first issue of our paper could make its appearance the famous Anarchist Squad of the Police Department handed to us a good dose of preventive efficiency. We withstood the siege in good humor, though it took two hours to dislocate the enemy from the trenches of our office. Still, we know now what to expect in the future. We rented an office from the Ess Ell Realty Co. from the first of December and settled down to work. Towards eve on December the 14th the guardians of peace clothed in civilian sheepskins made their appearance. They burst upon us with the cry: "Where is the stuff, hand it over to us." A homeric laughter was the answer. We inquired energetically whether the gentlemen took the precaution of securing a search warrant. "No." "Well, then there is nothing doing." The siege began. A burly spokesman of the Squad declared that they have an order to wait for the "Chief." The amiable bunch of blockheads settled down. None of us was allowed to leave the office except under the protection of a member of the Squad. After two hours of tedious waiting—we meanwhile continuing our work,—we were informed that the "Chief" had decided not to come. The clever spokesman was the Chief himself and we had a laugh on him.

The sequel: The following morning we were informed by the frightened landlord, an individual by the name of Frank, that we are undesirable tenants and that we have to vacate his place by the first of January. "Remember the explosion on Lexington avenue," cried this paste-board millionaire into our face. O shades of Caron, Berg and Hansen! If you did accomplish nothing else than to frighten all landlords of New York in their lower extremities, you deserve an imperishable monument in the heart of the workers.

The purpose: The game of the police is simply this. As they could not find any pretext for an arrest they used an underhanded and foul method to deprive us of our office. They hurt us materially for an amount of about fifty dollars. They didn't find any "stuff," for we are no children. Our "bombs" are made of a metal which couldn't penetrate into the skulls of these minions of stupidity.

To his Honor, Mayor Mitchel.

Sir:

The foregoing account of the action of the police towards THE REVOLT may seem a trifle to you, it may even amuse you. Still, we hope that you will spare a ... preach ... tango-time ... the consequences of such actions we are not willing to endure similar procedures at the hands of the Third Section of your Police Department.

Sir, remember that times and conditions change, but that the spirit of Liberty remains forever engraved in the hearts of the oppressed and downtrodden. Have you forgotten the memory of your grandfather, John Mitchel, the great Irish rebel, who was trapped by the Anarchist Squads of his time and sent as a felon to a prison in Australia?

Are you not satisfied with your achievements? So far we had brutal sluggers on the police force, we had sneaks, stool pigeons and traitors in the revolutionary movement, we had Pickertonians and Burnses, but you may glory in the thought that under your administration the system of *agent provocateurs* has been installed in the system of the police. You are the first magistrate in our commonwealth who had the questionable courage to approve of the pernicious activity of a Polignani.

Is this the efficiency you and your collaborators Wood and Bruere are so proud of? Does the College of John Harvard produce nothing else than hypocrites nowadays?

Notwithstanding all persecution the social rebellion of our days is marching on and the many methods of political upstarts will be able to roll back the high tide rushing towards the bulwarks of inequality.

War Is A Bore

ANYTHING that bores the public has no vitality. War is no longer interesting. Its spirit is gone. Its moral life has flown. It is stale. It begins and ends in the same old way. It is caused by the same old greed. It is nourished and maintained by the same old illusions. The same old scarecrows keep in existence its spiritually lifeless form. The same old hollow symbols cling to the tired ears of the multitude.

We are tired of drums and uniforms and hypocrisy decked out in noble phrases. We must be amused. This is no stall allow need. It is the need of all living things. Love amuses us. It is real to an emotion. It has meat. We seem able endlessly to vary the old theme. It is an illusion, we are eternally illusioned. We can play with it to the end of time. We can always build our dreams about it, our castles in the air.

But war is no longer amusing to the mind, nor to the fancy. We see through it. It is no longer an amusing illusion. It is a stale and unattractive reality, and a superficial and degrading reality. We no longer can inflame ourselves with grandiose sentiment about war. War is no longer sentimental. It is practical—for a few—very impractical for the many.

But the point is that we can no longer play with the idea of war, but when we do not play, seriously or lightly, we are bored. When the child does not

...ll. When the writer does not play, he ...ius, no life. When buildings are not put ...e same spirit as the child constructs, there architecture in them.

...erything that is alive entertains the mind, the ...ncy. War is no longer entertaining. Therefore it is dead—the spirit of it. The old buresome forms of it, dead remnants kept alive for evil purposes, weary as to extinction.

Sweep away the towering rubbish! Put by the stale old puppets, and seek more genuine play—play that has meaning to our modern nerves, to our subtler, more disillusioned civilization.

HUTCHINS HAPGOOD.

Parents: What Are They Good For?

WE are in the midst of a revolution of women. It is almost an accomplished fact. But in the great movements, economic and sexual, which are going on all over the world, there is one more revolution to be accomplished.

It is the revolt of the children against their parents. And that will be the most tremendous, the sublimest revolution of all.

It is time the truth was uttered about parents and their attitude toward those they bring into the world by an act of passion. It is time the mask of sentimental lies surrounding the sacredness of parents was slit into a thousand pieces and tossed back into the wardrobe-room of race-fakes.

Parents: What are they good for?

Let every man and woman look into the last recesses of his heart and answer that question fully.

Parents: What are they good for?

Let the squeezed, mutilated, shabby, humdrum, aching days of millions of youths and girls stand up and answer unashamedly.

Parents: What are they good for?

And billions of strangled, mutilated Minds and Passions and millions of shabby Days rise out of their tombs and answer: They should have been hanged before we grew into our sixth year.

Parents: Or the Mania for Mutilation. Millions of human beings might write a thesis with that for a title—a thesis that would make the horrors of a Dostoievsky seem merely a charivari.

Veiled beneath that vaunted sacred love of father and mother there lies a mania for mutilation which for pure diabolism is nowhere matched in nature.

Under the guise of a perpetual act of self-sacrifice the mother becomes the most inequitably selfish being that nature has yet created. Motherhood is nature's supreme diabolistic paradox.

It is always herself she fights for, and never for the child. It is always herself she dies for, and never for the sake of the child. Her love is the very frenzy and insanity of possession.

The father is greater than the mother, because his love-greed in regard to the offspring is not so cruel. Some father will even concede the right of a child to have opinions, ideas and sensations of its own. Motherhood can never ascend to that. It remains forever in the sties of self-worship.

Most children are born into a home. And by home I mean a death-cell. At the moment of birth the murderous machinations of the parents begin. Variation from the parent-type is the one thing to be ...ared. Hence the home. Hence the squirt-guns of ...ability, feigned godliness and prudery which begin their work on the senses and brain of the child just born. And when he first begins to smell it is the rotten stench of sanctity that greets his nostrils.

I accuse all parents of being liars every second in every hour in every day of their lives in the presence of their children.

I accuse every parent of a pantomime of hypocritical mummery from the day a child is born unto them.

I accuse every parent of conspiring against the unique vision and temperament that is born unto them.

I accuse every parent of spiritual mental, physical murder in seeking to gag the soul of the new-born and remould it in the image of one or both of them.

I accuse every parent of cowardice before the wide-open look of the child. They fake their personality from the very moment the child looks at them.

(No child ever knew its parents. No parent ever knew his or her child.)

I accuse parents of every physical and mental anguish that boys and girls suffer between the ages of thirteen and twenty.

(If parents only knew of the hate that enforced virgins feel for their parents, whose licentious and unrestrained practices in the marriage bond have obliterated their own early hatreds for their own parents.)

The home, the parent, must be protected at all costs!

Does a girl "go wrong" (that is, does she dare assert the rights of her womanhood and seek sanity away from the insane asylum for perverts called the respectable home?) The first thought in the minds of father and mother is the disgrace that will fall on THEM. A girl—a thing of flesh and blood—is being sacrificed to the Moloch of Respectability for the sake of the parents, those unrestrained and licentious parents, safe in the bosom of the marriage license!

The girl "went wrong"? No. The girl went right. Better one year of full surrender to love and passion and then death in the river than a life of respectable virginity and its inferno of agonies.

Does a boy "go wrong"? He gambles, he drinks, he seduces, he steals. Again the shriek through the cracking walls and falling roof of the House of Lies. "Our reputation! Our reputation! My God! Our reputation!"—that is the cry that mounts to the ironic topmost squat on the tottering chimney.

101

No parent ever showed sufficient respect for the child. Love—yes. Respect—never. That is because the love of the parent is the veil of selfishness and egotism, and respect involves self-sacrifice, an abasement in their own eyes of their supreme importance, a division of power.

Love is easier than respect and reaps a richer harvest of lies. To love a child involves no effort. To respect a child one must have ascended high in the scale of emotional and intellectual development.

The parent has no rights which the child is bound to respect. It is in the world without its own consent, bringing with it all the ills that flesh and mind are heir to.

Ancestors, environment, parents stand at the cradle like a menace of death. The social and economic systems under which a child is born have no rights which the child is bound to respect.

A mere flesh and blood asset of the parent and the blood sucking social and religiousts, which the child is shot—what should the spect?

ITS OWN SOUL ONLY!

The revolution of the child! The new Childrn. Crusade! This time they will march to rescue the own souls from the Unholy Sepulchre of their infidel parents.

Youths and maidens and children, you must soon write your Marseillaise. Stifled ones, strangled ones, mutilated ones, dutiful ones, suckled in the House of Fear and raised in the House of Craven Respectability or Leprous Poverty, the time approaches when each and every one must ask the heart:

My parents: What are they good for?

And your hearts will answer: Good for nothing until they are taught to respect, honor and obey us!

BENJAMIN DE CASSERES.

"What Are You Going to Do?"

ARE you hungry? Your mother, baby hungry? Are you desperate at sight of it? Do thoughts come that are strange and fearful, that make you feel as if you want to shrink back out of sight of men? For the thoughts that come are of robbery and maybe murder? You try to drive them away, but cannot, for they tell you that hunger is wrong and must not be!

You say you do not believe in robbery or murder, also, that the law of the land forbids it. This same law that makes hunger possible in the midst of plenty, that gives protection to the masters in robbing you of all that makes and means life, and so murders you in degrees (when not at once) to this law then you bow the knee, the head! How is it, do you respect murder when it comes in the form of the law, do you believe in it then?

You surely must, or if not, why continue to hunger, for you must know that hunger can be only because you are being robbed and murdered! Why then be quiet, is it because you fear the law, or what?

When hungry, possibly, for you it is sufficient to console yourself with the thought that you have obeyed the law.

Should you need a stronger sedative for stomach and mind, a greater, quieter robber of Will, you may kill, but you satisfy not hunger, nor your sense of justice (if you have any) but your cowardice, when you excuse yourself by saying you do not believe in robbery or murder for no reason whatsoever, be that reason even hunger!

But should war be declared and you are called upon to do murder, to kill and be killed, for what you are told and foolishly believe is your country, you hungry, homeless worker, what then? You have said that you do not believe in murder? But what is war if not murder? Is it not the most miserable kind of killing? You destroy not for yourself, but for others, for those that told you you must not kill when you were hungry. For they are one and the same; those who make the laws that deprive you of food, they also make and declare the wars that you are to fight in, die in, kill in! Should you obey them and enter the killing you would be worse than a dog, for even a dog refuses to fight for a master that starves him!

Do you fear to refuse because to do so means to be court-martialed and put to death! You think that would be foolish, that it would be better to go to the killing; there might be a possibility of your returning alive, whole or partly whole? And as to killing, why, all you have to do is to shoot up in the air? Well, that sounds like an excuse?

But what about your principle of no murder, do you uphold it, should you only pretend to take part in war, or do you think it is sufficient only to refuse to kill, and that to be killed for refusing is preferable to killing? Should you decide so again you would be a coward. To give up your life without a struggle to any power, be that power even the government, is as cowardly as to take the life or lives of those whom you have never seen and so can have nothing against. If to kill for other reason than self-defense is considered a crime by law even during a period of acknowledged war, the rulers then, themselves, fail to find an excuse for murder, for you see they restrict this murder known as War to just a certain place or people, to the killing of those whom it pleases them to have killed!

Then you be a man and refuse to either kill or be killed unless in self-defense. Show you understand what war means, and that you intend to protect yourself against it, and against those who would force you into it, in whatever shape or with whatever power they come.

That if you must either kill for the masters or be killed by them for refusing to kill and be killed, tell them that you shall fight and kill and die for your own life only!

GUSSIE MILLER.

The more fully and thoroughly we live, the more ready we are to sacrifice life for a single pleasurable emotion. people that lives and feels in this wise has no need of NIETZSCHE.

NOTE: Scanned issues of *Revolt* may be accessed at the Hippolyte Havel archive:

https://libcom.org/tags/hippolyte-havel

Publisher's Postscript

To the best of our knowledge, Benjamin DeCasseres' essay "Parents: What Are They Good For?" originally appeared exclusively in the premiere issue (dated January 1, 1916) of *Revolt*, a short-lived literary anarchist periodical that was published and edited by Hippolyte Havel in New York City before being suppressed by the U.S. government.[1]

Though it would be shut down after only eight issues, *Revolt* hit the ground as a journal of some distinction in the contemporaneous literature of resistance. In addition to DeCasseres' contributions (of which there would be six in total),[2] its pages featured letters by Bill Haywood and Margaret Sanger, poetry by Friedrich Nietzsche and Adolf Wolff, and texts by, *inter alia*, Thomas Paine, Clarence Lee Swartz, Max Weber,[3] Octave Mirabeau, Ralph Waldo Emerson, Walt Whitman, and Oscar Wilde. The *Revolt* "Advisory Board" consisted of Leonard D. Abbott, Elizabeth Gurly Flynn, Alexander Berkman, Harry M. Kelly, and Margaret H. Sanger.

Despite the publication's estimable stature within the early 20th century radical milieu, issues of *Revolt* were scarcely archived. Indeed, the present transcription (and facsimile reproduction) of DeCasseres' centerpiece essay comes to us from the only known microfilm collection, which has been digitized online as part of the Hippolyte Havel archive currently hosted by libcom.org.[4] Because this archive was assembled from extant print copies of *Revolt* that were generally in very poor condition, some sections of DeCasseres' source text are severely compromised in legibility, and some text is missing entirely due to rips in the original newsprint.

Preferring not to disrupt the foregoing reading experience with editorial flags and notes documenting such transcriptional uncertainties as they occur, I have opted instead to discreetly "fill in the gaps" without in-line commentary. In other words, I simply pored over the marred or missing text segments (in consultation with Kevin I. Slaughter, whose greater role in this project is noted below) and settled on contextually informed guesses. In lieu of conspicuously demarcative annotations, facsimile images of the scanned text segments have been clipped from the native source material and displayed on pages opposite their corresponding text as now construed and typeset. In addition to functioning as an unusual (and I hope visually engaging) juxtapository graphic element within the present layout, these offset images serve to provide readers with a straightforward means of comparing my interposed guesses with the raw source material "on the fly."

For broader context, readers are encouraged to consult the facsimile reproduction of the entire first issue of *Revolt* from which DeCasseres' now-titular essay has been transcribed. This document has been included as a supplement in the present volume (beginning at page 95), but it can be examined in granular detail online at the aforementioned Hippolyte Havel archive (where all eight issues of *Revolt* are freely available as PDF files).

With one maddeningly confounding exception (discussed in the endnote to this clause),[5] I am relatively confident in the accuracy of the interpolative guesswork entailed. Nevertheless, I am amenable to correction and welcome feedback from thoughtful readers who suspect my judgments to be amiss. Upon advice and consideration, revisions may be incorporated into subsequent printings of this book—and duly credited.

Until and unless another copy of *Revolt* #1 is discovered (and please let us know if you find one in your attic!), this is the best we can do.

WITH THAT MUCH AS BACKGROUND, I should add a few words specifically about this little book—the pocket-size curio that you are presently reading.

Although it bears the Nine-Banded Books colophon, I am delighted to acknowledge that *Parents: What Are They Good For?* is being released in solidarity with Kevin I. Slaughter's nonpareil Union of Egoists publishing and archival project, where it arrives as publication SA1252 in the Stand Alone catalog of troublesome tracts and sundry exhibits that resound within the variegated idiom of philosophical egoism.[6]

And of course, it was Kevin who brought the source essay to my attention, after which the idea to develop it for publication as a book—and in the form presently executed, more or less—latched almost intrusively, giving way to a small-scale passion project. There's not much of an origin story beyond that—although I suppose it's amusing to admit that my first thought was of the *Goops!* Seriously. Something about DeCasseres' essay jogged me to recall my childhood loathing for Gelett Burgess's misopedistic little rhyme-book,[7] and I remembered how my hatred rooted in a preliterate certainty that *the Goops were right!* In abducting Burgess's misunderstood moppets to "bookend" the festivities, my sentimental intention has been to affirm this precious childhood apostasy. Now liberated from their pedagogical provenance, *DeCasseres'* Goops are not impish brats in need of parental scolding and moral instruction; they are free spirits, insouciant rebels against all and nothing. Let them make noise.

Goop-centric grievances notwithstanding, I am pleased with this book. Yet I do understand that it is an *unusual* press production, given what has already been observed: that the core content consists of a single essay—and not a particularly long one! A reader might thus be forgiven for asking: *Why make it a book?* Why not publish it instead as a pamphlet? Or a broadside? Or a zine? Or perhaps as a chapter entry in an anthology? For that matter, why not just let it live on the internet? What is this gussied-up perfect-bound mockup, anyway? Some kind of *stunt*? A *gimmick*? A *concept*?

Mindful of L.A. Rollins' acid-tipped quip that "justification" is "just a fixation,"[8] I'll lay out what seems relevant. Because, despite the initial impression of novelty, the idea to present this century-plus-old essay in its present form—i.e., as a short book with paragraphs floating on individual pages—was crucially informed by my greater appreciation for DeCasseres' marque as a prosodist, rhapsodist, and polemicist; and even as a kind of philosopher.

Without going so far as to presume that *he would have done it this way*, I sincerely believe the present layout is tuned to DeCasseres' oratorical thrum and groove; that it serves to accentuate the beat-driven cadences and thematic inflections inherent in the source essay. In elevating the native text to its momentarily loftier stature as a price-of-admission exhibit, my foremost consideration has thus been to amplify—and in some sense, I suppose, why not, *glorify*—what I believe to have been DeCasseres' manifest intention, mainly by supplying a measure of breathing room for such lapidary locutions and grace notes and metric beats of stentorian intensity that, at least on my lasting impression, get muted in the typographic density of a conventionally block-set sequence of paragraphs.

Beyond formalistic indulgence, my posthumously privileged conceit to "make it a book" redounds to a broadly curatorial objective. I was delighted to discover this remarkable rant, and my frank hope is that the newly jazzed-up presentation will bring it some deserved attention. Surely there are manifestos against God and State that remain to be exhumed, and perhaps some that will yet make for lively reading in the 21st century. But while such terrain is well-trodden (and generally, let's be honest, redundant), DeCasseres' animadversion to *parental* authority still resonates as a bracingly provocative departure from the tacit strictures of rule-bound radicalism—a trespass, an upping of the anti-authoritarian ante.

Which would be enough reason to shout from the rooftops, no? Except I suspect the greater significance of this little essay that time forgot may turn on DeCasseres' ingenious apprehension of egoism (via Stirner) in salient relation to the grim logic of antinatalism (via Schopenhauer)—and without weepy-woe bullet-biting over the endgame. At the very least, that's a bold move. But I suspect it might also constitute a profoundly original philosophical inflection, perhaps too exquisitely (or brazenly!) expressed to have been noticed. If this wicked sleight of terminal insight didn't originate with DeCasseres, it has seldom since been intimated, much less articulated.[9]

So, in showcasing this essay as a stand-alone volume (and in the "Stand Alone" catalog, no less!), I mean to insist, without apology, that it deserves to be read and appreciated and contemplated—not just as a signature expression of DeCasseres' antinomian contrariety, but as a philosophical poem; a gauntlet cast into an abyss; a get-a-load-of-this humdinger. Vindication of the Goops.

A stunt, then. A gimmick. A concept. Fine. Made you look.

Chip Smith[10]
June 9, 2023

NOTES

1 As summarized by an anonymous contributor to the Hippolyte Havel archive hosted by libcom.org: "After the publication of the 7th issue, all 7 issues of *Revolt* were deemed 'unmailable' by the U.S. Postal Office (According to *Partisans of Freedom: A Study in American Anarchism* by William O. Reichert, the entire 7th issue of *Revolt* was locked up by the U.S. government, forcing Havel to issue the final issue clandestinely), as was the final issue upon its release. The journal survived less than four months, publishing its first article on January 1st, 1916 and it's final issue on March 11th, 1916." Source: https://libcom.org/article/revolt

2 This tally assumes that we are correct in our (confident) guess that the byline "ex nihilo nihil fit" is indeed DeCasseres' pseudonym. That alias, which would also appear as a phrase in DeCasseres' book *Raiders of the Absolute*, is credited to a text entitled "The Overlord" that was published the seventh (penultimate) issue of *Revolt*. The five contributions explicitly attributed to DeCasseres are: "Parents: What Are They Good For?" (Vol I No. 1); "The Liberation of Man" (Vol. I No. 3); "Potporri"(Vol. I No. 4); "Three Moralities" (Vol. I No. 5); and "Pierrot—Parabrahma"(Vol. I No. 6).

3 The American artist, not the German sociologist. Famously a Cubist painter, Weber was also a poet whose second collection of poetry, *Primitives: Poems and Woodcuts* (Spiral Press, 1926; reprinted by the Union of Egoists as SA1235 in September, 2022) featured an introduction by Benjamin DeCasseres. (Fun fact: in 1913 DeCasseres announced his bid for mayor of New York City as a "Cubist Candidate," vowing, among other things, to "legalize human frailties.") One of Weber's poems can be seen on page 99 of this volume, appearing just a couple of pages before DeCasseres' showcase essay in the facsimile reproduction of *Revolt* #1.

4 See: https://libcom.org/tags/hippolyte-havel

5 The notable exception, as careful readers will have observed, concerns the paragraph that now appears as an offset text segment on page 75 of the present volume. As can be seen by reference to the scanned clipping on the preceding (verso-opposite) page, the damage to the corresponding section of the source document was, in this instance, significant enough to confound reasonable efforts at a confident transcription. The stand-in text now in place was ultimately decided by Nine-Banded Books publisher Chip Smith (me), who, to his (my) dubious credit, obsessed over the missing words for the better part of three days before settling, with profound misgivings, on the present result—which is almost certainly wrong!

Without dwelling at interminable length on the factors informing this hopeless guess, it should be noted that the deliberative process entailed: 1) a metric appraisal of the typographic space affected (roughly 11 crucial character spaces, plus or minus one in consideration of kerning); 2) contextual clues that the missing text probably included a preposition; 3) a review of relevant style, usage, and word choices evident in online archival sources of Benjamin DeCasseres' writings; 4) the presence of a possibly residual typographic element following the lost word beginning with "s" suggesting that the next letter might be characterized by a baseline descender; and 5) due attention to grammatical (or poetic) agreement (or consonance).

Regarding factor 3 above, I determined that De-Casseres rather liked variants of the word "scheme," and I strongly considered that the elusive "s" word might be "schemes" (thus, "…blood sucking social and religious *schemes*…"). My eventual substitution of "system" followed only after some nagging reconsideration of factor 4—i.e., in positing the shaky assumption that the seeming bit of residual type following the "s" is best interpreted as evidence of a baseline descending characteristic in the next letter. Observing that the letter "y" satisfied this criterion in a manner consistent with its appearance elswhere in the source text, I reluctantly settled on "system" as the least presumptuous "sy" word that adhered to context. I still prefer "schemes," however, which is why I am including this "CYA" paragraph as a caveat in my account.

Ultimately, the choice of the present (again, probably wrong) stand-in text hinged largely on granting, *in arguendo*, the tentative—yet embarrassingly epiphanic—presumption that the word "shot," in the context of the problem paragraph ("...the child is shot") was not, as a cursory reading might suggest, intended as a verb denoting the act of shooting or being shot, but rather as a *noun* specifically (semi-archaically/poetically) likening the child to an expendable source of ammunition or fodder, such that might be deployed in the service of a "blood sucking social and religious [~~schemes~~ system]." The resulting roadwork, while perhaps less than syntactically satisfying, does suggest a prose-poetic, if not strictly metonymic, symmetry of concepts, with the child being descried at once as a "blood asset" to the parents and as another kind of asset ("shot," meaning essentially "cannon fodder") for a vampiric "system" with which "the parent" is complicitously allied. The child, at both metaphorical turns, is depicted as means rather than an end.

Hermeneutics be damned, this lays bare the diligence done. Blame me! And have at it, sleuths.

6 For an up-to-date list, click the "Stand Alone" menu option at: www.unionofegoists.com

7 Since my wife insists that "nobody remembers the Goops!," I should clarify that I am referring primarily to Gelett Burgess's 1900 book, *Goops and How to Be Them: A Manual of Manners for Polite Infants Inculcating Many Juvenile Virtues Both by Precept and Example, with Ninety Drawings*. Revisiting Burgess's larger body of work through various public domain archives as an adult, I'm more inclined to believe his intentions were somewhat tongue-in-cheek—or that his resitation of Victorian moral instruction can be seen as obliquely, or perhaps subversively, satirical. Regardless, this was *not* how the book was popularly promoted or received even in the early 1970s, when my wicked* grandmother reprimanded me with Goop verses.

(*I use the term "wicked" advisedly. Worse than a Christian scold, my paternal "mamaw" was almost certainly a serial practitioner of infanticide. Long story. Buy me a drink someday and I'll tell you all about it.)

8 Look for the "(Re)Expanded and Revised" edition of *Lucifer's Lexicon*, co-published by Nine-Banded Books and Underworld Amusements in 2020. Definition of "Justification."

9 Currently fashionable commie-coded iterations of "family abolitionism" merely kick the can down the road, don't they? Same with "my generation"-branded revolutionary catcalls of whichever complexion. Contemporary antinatalist gestures, while more relevant, omit the corollary element of egoism that distinguishes and animates DeCasseres' gravamen. Nearer to the fire, perhaps—yet oh-so distant still—might be Seana Shiffrin's legal-philosophical disquisitions on "wrongful life" as a radical cause of action. Parents as existential tortfeasors, oh my. So sue them!

10 This "Postscript" was composed in collaboration with Kevin I. Slaughter, whose contribution is hereby gratefully acknowedged. The editorial bloviations, however, are mine alone.

BenjaminDecasseres.com

Who's Who

in

AMERICAN JEWRY

DE CASSERES, BENJAMIN:

Author; b. Apr. 3, 1873, Phila., Pa. (collateral descendant of Benedict (Baruch) de Spinoza); s. David and Charlotte (Davis) De Casseres; ed. Public Schools of Phila. until 12 years of age; self-educated; m. Bio Terrill (granddaughter of Stephen Mack and Princess Ho-no-ne-gah, Daughter of the Amer. Revolution), Oct. 12, 1919, N. Y. Poet, essayist, thinker and satirist. With Phila. Press, 1889-99; N. Y. Sun, 1899-1903; N. Y. Herald, 1903-06; co-founder and editorial writer, El Diario (City of Mexico, 1906-07); N. Y. Herald, 1907-19; staff of Famous Players-Lasky Corp., 1920-23; head of title dept., Universal Pictures Corp. (Hollywood). 1924-25; free-lance writer, book reviews, special articles and dramatic critic for Arts and Decoration, 1926. Has contributed to N. Y. Times, Herald Tribune, The Sun, Theatre Magazine, Amer. Mercury (one of founders-subscribers), The Philistine, Internatl. Book Review, the Forum, Life, Judge, Puck, L'en Dehors (Orleans, France), the Amer. Hebrew and the Jewish Exponent. Author: The Mirrors of New York (stories and essays), 1925; The Shadow Eater (poems), 1915, Chameleon; Being the Book of My Selves, 1922; James Gibbons Huneker, 1925; Forty Immortals, 1925; Litanies of Negation, 1926, and fifteen other unpublished books of satire, philosophy and poetry. Work translated into French by Remy de Gourmont; work has been acclaimed for its originality and daring. Member: The Authors' League of Amer.; Authors' Guild of Amer.; Spinoza Soc. Club: Newspaper. Address: 131 E. 19th St., N. Y. City.

1926

UnionOfEgoists.com

STAND ALONE

SA1000: EN MARGE No. 1 (May 2016) • SA1005: For Love and Money (July 2016) • SA1010: The Martyrdom of Percy Whitcomb (October 2016) • SA1015: The Eagle and the Serpent Index of Names (December 2016) • SA1017: Sidney E. Parker 1993 Interview (January 2017) • SA1019: Max Stirner/Roots of the Right (February 2017) • SA1020: Philosophy of Time (March 2017) • SA1023: Egoism: The First Two Volumes 1890–1892 (April 2017) • SA1025: Benjamin DeCasseres Ephemera (May 2017) • SA1027: "I" Vol. 1 No. 1 (June 2017) • SA1029: "Benjamin DeCasseres, Sidney E. Parker, Voltairine de Cleyre" (July 2019) • SA1030: A Critique of Anarchist Communism (August 2017) • SA1033: The Right to Ignore the State (September 2017) • SA1035: The Walford–Parker Exchange (November 2017) • SA1050: The Eagle and The Serpent Vol. 2 No. 5 (January 2018) • SA1055: Max Stirner's Egoism and Nihilism (February 2018) • SA1060: What is Man's Destiny? (March 2018) • SA1065: The Cynic's Breviary (April 2018) • SA1068: The Absolute Elsewhere (May 2018) • SA1070: Rebuilding the World (June 2018) • SA1075: Elbert Hubbard's The Philistine (July 2018) • SA1080: Little Handbook of Individualism (August 2018) • SA1081: "To Hell with DeCasseres!" (September 2018) • SA1083: The New En Marge (September 2018) • SA1084: Courage by Bart Kennedy (September 2018) • SA1085: Liberty Tables of Content (October 2018) • SA1087: Secret Patreon Exclusive (November 2018) SA1088: A Stuffed Club T-Shirt (November 2018) • SA1090: Protagoras. Nietzsche. Stirner. (December 2018) • SA1095: The Nietzsche Movement in England (January 2019) • SA1107: Anarchism and Individualism (March 2018) • SA1110: BOVARYSM: The Art-Philosophy of Jules de Gaultier (April 2018) • SA1111: "As I See: Nietzsche" (May 2019) • SA1113: Covington Hall's Satanic Lumberjacks & Southron Rebels (June 2018) • SA1115: Ludovici's Zarathustra (July 2019) • SA1120: Max Stirner Versus Karl Marx (August 2019) • SA1125: The New En Marge Vol. 2 No. 1 (September 2019) • SA1127: A Brave and Beautiful Spirit: Dora Marsden, 1882–1960 (September 2019) • SA1129: UoE Logo Lapel Pin (October 2019) • SA1130: The False Principle of Our Education (November 2019) • SA1131: The Boy of Bethlehem (December 2019) • SA1133: The Superman in America (January 2020) • SA1135: With Claw and Fang (February 2020) • SA1137: Dora Marsden Bibliography (March 2020) • SA1140: The Illusion of Anarchism (April 2020) • SA1145: La 'Bande à Bonnot' (May 2020) • SA1150: I Beheld Redbeard: An Interview with Darrell W. Conder (October 2020) • SA1155: Ink-Stained Imp and the Pugilist Painter (August 2020) • SA1160: Dora Marsden: Vida y obra (September 2020) • SA1170: "Might is Right" Lapel Pin (November 2020) • SA1172: Hyde Park Orator Illustrated, Hardback (December 2020) • SA1175: Hyde Park Orator Illustrated, Paperback (January 2021) • SA1180: The Individualist by Ben DeCasseres (February 2021) • SA1185: The Gospel of Power (March 2021) • SA1190: Against Words: A Dora Marsden Sketchbook (April 2021) • SA1200: Works of DeCasseres Vol. 1 (May 2021) • SA1201: Works of DeCasseres Vol. 2 (June 2021) • SA1201: Works of DeCasseres Vol. 2 (July 2021) • SA1205: Might is Right: 1927 Facsimile & Leaf Edition (August 2021) • SA1210: On Active Service (September 2021) • SA1215: Voluntary Socialism (October 2021) • SA1217: Man-Eating and Man-Sacrificing (November 2021) • SA1220: "TYPE" Letterpress Broadside (December 2021) • SA1221: Max Stirner: Especial Frases (January 2022) • SA1225: Max Stirner and the Philosophy of the Individual (March 2022) • SA1227: Speaker's Corner Anthology (May 2022) • SA1230: Immorality as a Philosophic Principle (July 2022) • SA1235: Primitives (September 2022) • SA1245: The Communist–Parasite State (November 2022) • SA1246: Individual Action at Archive.org (January 2023) • SA1247: Max Stirner and the German Followers of Proudhon (March 2023) • SA1250: The Radical Book Shop of Chicago (April 2023) • **SA1252: Parents: What Are They Good For? (June 2023)** • [Ongoing...]

Caveat Lector.

www.NineBandedBooks.com